The Fear in Me

The Inner-Self Series

Author
Tricia Khan

Illustrator
Nataliia Tymoshenko

This book belongs to:

_____

Fear is SCARY,
Fear makes me weary.

When I'm fearful, I feel stuck.
With fear, I have no luck.

Everywhere I go,
everything I do,
fear sticks to me
like glue.

It shadows over me in the dark of the night;
when all I want to do is shine bright as a light.

I run because of fear.
I hide because I'm scared.

I cry when fear stands
in front of me.
I quiver when it takes
control of me.

When I'm fearful,
I can't be true to myself;
I curl up like a snail
in its shell.

Fear is a thought that's in my head.
It plays with my mind when I'm in bed.

"Fear is my enemy,
it's not my friend.
It has me at my wit's end.

I am tired of being fearful;
I will show fear no more.
I will look fear in the face
and say, ...

I will stand up tall,
I will break the wall.
I will release fear
and not answer its call.

Now, I can be strong.
I can do anything and know I belong.
And if fear tries to strike,
I will still do the things I like.

I will walk to school,
with my head held high.
I will be brave;
when a bee flies by.

I will go to class completely prepared.
Present my ideas without feeling scared.
And, the more I try to do new things,
my inner fears will grow real thin.

I will step out in faith.
I will believe in me.
I will become whatever I want to be.
And, once I let go and believe in myself.
Then fear can't control me or anyone else.

Bye-bye!

P-O-O-F!!.
P-O-O-F!.,
P-O-O-F!!.
P-O-O-F.,
P-O-O-F!.,

Goodbye, fear, can't you
see, I've released you,
now I am free.

Amazon

Instagram

www.ingramcontent.com/pod-product-compliance
Lightning Source LLC
Chambersburg PA
CBHW042132070426

42450CB00002BA/89